Cabins & Camps

Cabins & Camps

Written & Photographed by RALPH KYLLOE

Gibbs Smith, Publisher
Salt Lake City

"If we all did the things we are capable of doing,
we would literally astound ourselves."

— Thomas A. Edison

First Edition
15 14 13 12   9 8
Copyright © 2002 by Ralph Kylloe

Published by
Gibbs Smith, Publisher
P.O. Box 667
Layton, Utah 84041

Orders: 1-800-748-5439
www.gibbs-smith.com

Designed by Barry Hansen
Printed and bound in Hong Kong

Library of Congress Cataloging-in-Publication Data

Kylloe, Ralph R.
Cabins and camps / written and photographed by Ralph Kylloe.— 1st ed.

p. cm.
ISBN 1-58685-135-7
1. Log cabins—Decoration. 2. Decoration and ornament, Rustic. 3. Vacation homes. I. Title.
NK2195.L63 K97 2002
728.7'3'0973—dc21
2002008534

Contents

Acknowledgments

WHEN I PUBLISHED *Rustic Artistry for the Home* (Gibbs Smith, Publisher, 2000), I felt that I had completed the definitive book on rustic style. Times and minds change. Rustic furniture builders create new things. New rustic homes are built. Undiscovered antique pieces are found—and people and publishers want more.

So I began working on this book in the spring of 2001. To photograph the book, I traveled to Maine, Vermont, Connecticut, New Hampshire, Michigan, Indiana, Colorado, Montana, Wyoming, Idaho, and California. I also called upon considerable resources in my home area of upstate New York. As always, there are many people to thank for their efforts in helping me to complete this book. I am certain that I have forgotten several people who should have been mentioned here. So from the start I apologize for my oversight (it's tough to get old!).

First and foremost, I thank the gracious people who allowed me to photograph their homes; most of them prefer to remain anonymous.

I absolutely need to thank the following: Colt and Kathy Bagley; Barney, Susan and Erin Bellinger; George and Mary Jacques; Doug and Janice Tedrow; Lester "Motorcycle Man" Santos; Jack Leadley; Chris Wager; Peter Winter; Randy Holden; Lori Toledo; John Bennett; Peter Bizzare; Veronica Nemethy; Diana Beattie; John Slingerland; Matt and Gussy Madsen; Tim Duncan; Brian Kelly; Marvin "Pinky" O'Dell; Jorma and Vanessa Kaukonen; Jack Casady; Ann Tillotson Miller; Michael Bird; Barbara and Thad Collum; Robby Secor; Chester Prouty; Alice Booth; Mike and Terry Griffin; Jerry and Jessica Farrell; Charlie Brown; John Skinner; Tim Groth; Michael and Kathleen Byrne; Melissa Greenauer; John Blangiardo; Harry Howard at Yellowstone Traditions; Tom and Bill Welsh; Tina Bradt; Peter Lee; John and Joanne Lefner; Sandy and Terry Winchell; Jimmy and Linda Covert; Ron and Jean Shanor; Marvin Davis; Bob and Judy Oestreicher; David Medwin; David and Edye Fagensen; Michael and Kim Cantanucci; Chris Williams; Tom Weiskopf; Heidi Weiskopf; Larry Pearson; Greg Lemond; and Cheryl Gallagher. Along with lawyers and dentists, editors are at the top of the "dislike and can't stand" list for all writers and photographers. Quite to the contrary, my editor, Madge Baird, vice president at Gibbs Smith, Publisher, is an absolute sweetheart. She definitely keeps me in line, keeps my writing from rambling all over the place, tolerates my moodiness, and definitely helps clarify what I'm trying to say with my photos and writings. Thank you, Madge! I also thank my wife, Michele, and daughter, Lindsey. Michele helps style many of my photos and travels with me around the country. She also runs my design and gallery business. I could not do what I do without her. My daughter helps by putting her fingerprints on the lenses of my cameras whenever possible. God bless her!

Finally, a special thanks to Gibbs Smith. Through his many books at Gibbs Smith, Publisher, he has been more than instrumental in keeping both the western and rustic spirit alive. Thank you, Gibbs!

Preface

I BOUGHT MY FIRST SERIOUS PIECE of rustic furniture in 1978 while I was a doctoral student at Boston University. My roommate at the time, Jon Ames, was in the antiques business. He brought home a gorgeous six-foot oval dining room table with massive log legs. It was signed Old Hickory Chair Company. I bought it from him for $280, which was about my life savings at the time. A month later, he bought it back from me for $400. At that moment, I knew there was something to the antiques business. It was the quickest $120 dollars I have ever made!

During time away from my studies, I hung out with Jon and learned the business. In time, I finished my studies and eventually went on to Harvard University at nights for another degree in management. Although I trained as an academic, the thought of being inside at a desk the rest of my life was not thrilling. The art world had become my passion. I loved the treasure hunt, the yard sales and flea markets, the old houses, the auctions, the freedom of the road, and being my own boss.

My first real score was at a junk flea-market sale. I purchased three small bags of costume jewelry for two dollars. That afternoon, a jewelry dealer paid me a thousand dollars for the three bags of jewelry, which contained three diamond rings, several gold bands, and other stuff. That was it—I was hooked! There was no looking back.

But I had no interest in jewelry—I kept thinking about that Old Hickory table. A year later, I took a one-semester teaching position at Purdue University in Indiana. On weekends I traveled the back roads to yard sales and auctions and found hickory furniture everywhere. I soon realized that Indiana, especially Martinsville, was the Mecca for hickory furniture. Library research turned up certain information, but I learned the most from visiting retirement homes in Martinsville. There I met numerous individuals who had worked for several of the companies that had built hickory furniture in the earlier part of the twentieth century. Indiana has the friendliest and most loquacious people in the country. Their stories were insightful and fascinating. In time, I learned that Indiana boasted ten different companies manufacturing hickory furniture, beginning in 1892 with the Old Hickory Chair Company in Martinsville.

I started to amass a serious collection of hickory furniture. I am certain that I knocked on every door in Indiana looking for the stuff. I had no shame! Within a year I had purchased more than seven hundred pieces, which I stored in a huge four-story barn in Massachusetts. Things were cheap at that time. I could buy great sets of chairs for a few hundred dollars, porch swings for two hundred, rockers and armchairs for about seventy-five dollars. In one small town, I found a motel that was going out of business and paid the owner five hundred dollars for forty hickory beds, fifteen hickory bureaus, mirrors, coat stands, tables, and more stuff than I had ever had!

But I was now seriously in debt. I had maxed out several credit cards and payments were coming due. The trouble was that no one else in the world shared my vision of how wonderful rustic furniture really was. I set up at several major antiques shows in New York City. Many people laughed at my furniture and me. I had no taste, they said. Business was poor to nonexistent. My wife at the time thought I was crazy (I'm certain that she still does—and there is probably some truth to the notion!), and she promptly divorced me. My mother constantly reminds me that I have fifteen years of college behind me and I sell stick furniture for a living. "What a waste," she says.

A few years went by and I eked out a living. But then in the early eighties, rustic caught on. I started decorating high-end stores like Polo and Timberland. Next was Harrods of London, Disney, and then Orvis, L. L. Bean, and Macy's windows at Christmastime. I started renting furniture to movie production companies and theatre groups. And it wasn't only furniture. In the settings I included fishing creels, old skis and snowshoes, canoe paddles, oars, and early Old Town canoes. Lanterns, bamboo fishing poles, Adirondack pack baskets, and taxidermy were also in demand. I added colorful textiles such as camp blankets and Indian rugs to give life and energy to the settings. Then I started decorating restaurants and private residences—huge ones and many of them. I set up museum exhibits in Boston, Montreal, and Indianapolis and contributed numerous pieces to other museums in New York City. I started sending high-end pieces all over the world to clients who flew in just to see me! Over the years, magazines such as *Country Living* and *Architectural Digest* photographed my home, and I wrote dozens of articles for many publications. The state of Indiana awarded me a significant grant to write the history of the Indiana hickory furniture movement, and I have spoken hundreds of times before design and architecture groups. I appeared on TV many times and the *Today Show* broadcast from my gallery in 1999.

Photographic Comments

My undergraduate degree is in photography. I have been a student of both photographic technology and the art of the photography for more than thirty-five years. During my early years as a photographer, I used all the technology I could get my hands on—strobes, power packs, fill lights—you name it, I used it. But in recent years I have come to dislike the artificial effects that technology creates. Artificial light causes settings to appear too flat. That's not how things actually look at all. I want to see on the printed page what's real, what the eye actually sees on-site. I want to see depth and contours. When absolutely necessary I still use an occasional fill light, but I've been using only existing light only for the past few years. I like the shadows and shades that natural sunlight creates.

Decorating Comments

There are several approaches to decorating. I'll begin with my own approach, which I happily call "chaotic" or "neurotic." I believe that one can never have enough stuff. And I believe in filling up every last inch of wall, ceiling, and floor space with great collections. (For an example, see Kamp Kylloe, featured in this book.) I have over five hundred small birch bark picture frames in my collection, and whenever I see another, I have to have it. I also collect paddles, Adirondack pack baskets, creels, nets, old photos, and all kinds of other rustic stuff. Whenever I come home from a major flea market, I spread everything out in my home and gallery and leave it there until my wife insists that I find places for my "treasures." (Don't forget that recently General Norman Schwarzkopf said that his eleventh commandment is that one can "never have enough fishing poles." The general is a very wise man!)

Realistically, in a clinical sense, I—and millions of other collectors—probably have a serious compulsive/obsessive disorder. I frequently will drive five hundred miles for the opening of an antiques show or sit for hours at an auction and wait until the item that I want comes up. I hate losing and will go to any length to own something. Several years ago a great rustic twig mosaic desk came up at a Maine auction. I said to myself that I would be willing to pay up to four thousand dollars for it, but when it came up, I bid the piece to well over twenty thousand dollars and still didn't get the desk! I sulked about it for weeks. But life goes on.

For sanity's sake, it's necessary to make order out of chaos. So, here are two bits of sound decorating advice:

- When hanging things on walls, big things go on the bottom and small things go on top.
- Tell stories with your arrangements.

Most normal people find the chaotic approach a bit overdone, so on many projects my wife and I use the "monastic" approach. Used frequently in projects other than log cabins, this style is much calmer and more soothing than the all-or-nothing look. Single items or just a few well-placed ones become focal points with the right accent light or eye-catching color. Featuring pieces or vignettes that correlate with the personalities of the owners can really make a personal statement. Whatever you collect, one thing is critical—and please take me seriously on this: It is far better to buy a few really great things than to gather a larger quantity of questionable value. You don't need a thousand twig stands in your house to make it look rustic. Spend the extra money to buy something of quality and you'll forever be happy with your investment.

Exordium

I'VE BEEN TOLD THAT I HAVE BEEN A KEY PLAYER in the rustic revival, with my gallery business and books. I may have played a small part, but rustic furniture and settings have been with us for generations. It is nothing new. Many other people, such as Bob Doyle from Lake Placid, New York, and Terry and Sandy Winchell from Jackson, Wyoming, were incredibly instrumental years ago in popularizing rustic pieces as well.  At present I own a large 7,500-square-foot log cabin gallery in the Adirondacks of upstate New York. I am involved in all kinds of projects, from designing residences and commercial buildings to selling high-end rustic furniture, building custom-made furniture in our workshops, lecturing around the country in front of a variety of audiences, and writing on the subject. Many people call my shop wanting appraisals of their furniture, quotes on custom orders, or to sell me their latest creation. Callers often ask for advice concerning their home's construction or design and other things related to rustic décor and lifestyle.

This structure is covered with bark-on hemlock siding. Moose antlers crown the entryway. Although commonly used in such fashion, antlers are often chewed upon by all sorts of creatures for their salts and other nutrients. This pair of moose antlers lost a good two inches in the first week after I applied them to the front entrance of my summer cabin. The local squirrels not only had a gourmet feast on the antlers but also stripped the bark off my new bark-on cedar railing. To this date I have no solution to the problem!

*Detail of bark-on hemlock siding.
In order for the bark to remain on
the wood, the logs must be cut
during the cold months, when the
sap is not running.*

*By dividing an exterior wall
into a grid, the builder of
this home worked around the
size limitations of sheeted
birch bark to create a classic
Adirondack-style facade.*

Aged and weathered Adirondack siding.

Here are my responses to the most frequently asked questions:

🏠 Cut in the winter (October through December), and the bark stays on. Cut in the summer, and the bark falls off. It's that simple. Many people around the country, including designers, architects, and contractors, have either made bark-on furniture or have placed bark-on logs in their homes for structural or aesthetic purposes. Unfortunately, if the material was cut at the wrong time of the year, the bark will fall off. One architect was so distraught about this situation with the massive logs he had placed in a client's home that he hired a caretaker to set up ladders and glue bark that had fallen off back onto the logs—once a month! And this has been going on for fifteen years!

🏠 If you are going to use raw or fresh-cut wood for projects, it has to be dry. That means the moisture content must be around 7 percent. If it's higher than that, the wood will shrink.

🏠 Wood, specifically logs, checks and splits. There is nothing you can do about it. The drier the logs, the less checking will occur. If you do not like checked logs, you can fill the cracks with caulking or cover the inside walls with Sheetrock.

🏠 Occasionally, regardless of how careful we are, furniture and logs may become infested with insects. Small mounds of sawdust are telltale signs of powder-post beetles. But beetles aren't the only ones that create sawdust. Termites and carpenter ants will do the same. One cure is to place the piece of furniture outside and spray the infected area with insecticide. Another solution is to spray the bug holes with WD-40. (Remember to use caution in handling all chemicals.)

If the problem persists, call your local exterminator. Insects are not a problem to be ignored.

🏠 Furniture does not belong outside, where it will be exposed to rain, snow, direct sunlight, or other harsh environmental elements. Some woods, such as cedar and teak, may last for extended periods outside, but more furniture has been lost to the elements than to anything else. Some people argue that coating rustic furniture with spar varnish or paint makes it last indefinitely, but regardless, I suggest that one use caution when leaving rustic furniture in direct exposure to the elements.

🏠 An understanding of the historical context of rustic furniture will give you grounding when discussing rustic décor or buying rustic furniture. The vast majority of furniture that we call Adirondack style (bark on) was made in Indiana by one of ten different companies. Hickory furniture was made in Indiana, not in the Adirondacks. And just because it has bark on it doesn't mean that it was made by Old Hickory. I have been offered thousands of twig stands, cedar chairs, willow benches, and cypress tables by owners guaranteeing me that their "treasures" were made by Old Hickory. Buyer beware: about 98 percent of the furniture made by Old Hickory bears their brand or paper label. If it doesn't bear such a brand, it likely isn't Old Hickory.

🏠 Decorators, designers, architects, and rustic aficionados love white birch bark for a simple reason: it's quite beautiful. But here is a caution: while the bark from white birch trees makes great covering for furniture and accessories, the actual wood from white birch trees is very unstable. It decays and rots quickly. It should not be used for banisters, railings, newel posts, stringers, table legs, bedposts, or other functional items. After a few years, the joints will loosen, resulting in wobbly tables and shaky beds and railings. Yellow birch is a stable alternative to white.

In Praise of Originality

We sell hundreds of pieces of high-end furniture every year. It is a real problem keeping the store full. Just about every day someone comes by with a load of furniture to sell. Or I receive photos in the mail from people wanting an opinion on their efforts. Most of the craftsmen and -women are amateurs hoping to break into the rustic furniture business. In general, I want to be encouraging and offer tips on how to improve their efforts. I usually invite builders in to see the works of others that have achieved a high level of craftsmanship. In my files are photos of thousands of pieces of furniture from hundreds of rustic furniture builders.

Most people think it's easy to build rustic furniture. It's not. It's time-consuming and difficult. Anyone can pound a few nails together, but to create a piece of artwork is another story. Extraordinary patience, passion, skill, and effort are required. I tell this to everyone: Do not make copies of others' work. There's no art in that. In truth, there is very little

The interior walls of this very comfortable rustic retreat have been covered with Adirondack siding, also called wavy board, brain storm, or pig pen siding.

Below left: Bark-on cedar railings after squirrels and other creatures had stripped them for nesting material.

Bark-on hemlock siding.

Above: The owner of this home, an architect, incorporated large sheets of birch bark into the siding of this structure.

Board-and-batten siding. The half-cut logs are hemlock. Note traces of bark beetles.

new under the sun. It is both important and necessary to learn a trade or skill from others. Regardless of the direction we take in our lives, we are all influenced by each other. Nonetheless, no one ever became famous or rich by making knock-offs. There is no doubt that the world is in a constant state of change. Our present economic system both requires and allows for this, but we do not progress as individuals or as a species unless we constantly strive for originality and uniqueness in our efforts. At the same time, if you think that you are an originator of a certain element within the rustic furniture business, consider again. As a furniture historian, I can assure you that someone somewhere has already done it or made it.

On the other hand, don't hit the ceiling and threaten lawsuits if someone makes something similar to yours. Each piece of wood—the shape of the branches and limbs used—gives each piece of furniture some originality. Take it as a compliment if someone tries to duplicate your work, and then go and build something new. Competition keeps us on our toes and forces us to strive for new ideas. We all grow as a result. Remember this: Complacency is the antecedent to mediocrity. If you don't constantly improve your products and develop new designs, you'll be left behind.

With a bit of maturation comes the realization that the opinions of others are, in reality, just not that important. Monuments were never built to critics; monuments were built to people who do things. Talk is cheap. Follow the voices you hear. Build great furniture. Be an artist. Improve your life.

On Nature and Rustic

In 1969, C. A. Weslager wrote that "the modern family is so far removed in its thoughts and surroundings from the home-spun life of earlier generations of Americans that it is easy to overlook the reality and significance of the log cabin as a home" (*The Log Cabin in America: From Pioneer Days to the Present,* Rutgers University Press).

A lot has happened since 1969. Wars, computers, the Hubble telescope, the mapping of the human genome, the Internet, terrorism, and scientific breakthroughs that were just a dream a few decades earlier have shaped our current world and existence.

A few rats in a box, and tranquility prevails. Too many rats in a box, and chaos and violence ensue. This is a well-known and well-documented fact. It is, unfortunately, a reality. Many living in today's world are required to reside in towering cathedrals and urban sprawl. But in our hearts we are nomads. For millions of generations we moved with the seasons and followed the calls of the wild. When the animals moved, we followed them. When the salmon arrived, we made certain that we were at the water's edge. When the ice came, we sought warmer climates. Just imagine a people traveling across the dry land between Russia and North America. Imagine traveling from Alaska to Key West and never seeing another human, a fence, telephone line, or road. Imagine fishing and hunting every day. Imagine sixty million buffalo and flocks of birds so immense that the sky would darken when they flew. Imagine a thousand miles of brilliant wildflowers, forests of immense trees pointing to the heavens, clear air and clean water. Imagine not knowing what new adventures each day would bring. Imagine having all your possessions on your back. Imagine no taxes, no traffic jams, no arsenic, anthrax, lawsuits, insurance claims, or paperwork.

Are we happier today than we were a few thousand years ago? I suspect that in some respects we probably are. Frankly, I am happy to know that if I get a toothache or a broken arm, I can turn to someone for help. I like knowing how the universe began. I like peering through a microscope and understanding (at a very basic level) how the body works. I like having outlets for a variety of creative impulses. I like having information at my fingertips. Our technology, so awe-inspiring and profound, is the result of creative urges, a quest for answers and solutions. There is a very profound beauty in solutions. But somewhere inside my head (and maybe the heads of others as well) I hear tiny voices compelling me to gaze at mountains, ponder the mysteries of flowing water, revel in and be hypnotized by dancing fire, marvel at passing clouds. I get chills when I hear elk bugle and feel humbled when I stroll beneath the redwoods. Perhaps my most memorable day was when, during a fishing trip to Alaska, I was surrounded by seven adult brown bears who casually fed on salmon that raced by my feet in their quest to travel the last few miles of their life's journey. I could hear the bears breathing. I could hear them breaking the bones of fish. I was mesmerized. It was very real and I was very much alive during the experience. Rustic structures and rustic furniture do that to me as well. Nature is so honest. I love the sensual curves and the freedom of roots and branches. I love the fact that trees and plants of all kinds fought against tremendous odds to survive and grow.

To preserve log structures from the elements, homeowners often paint them. Nature's colors honor the rustic ambience.

This interesting resort in Ketchum, Idaho, uses multiple colors to enhance and differentiate.

The burls, knots, and contortions are outside the perils and dogmas of society. Trees don't have the same headaches I do. I envy them. I envy their peace. I touch the trees. I feel good when I'm around them. I find refuge there. I find new strength and a reason to go on. Many of us try to listen to the voices in our heads—voices that help us find meaning. But the voices are often subtle and not easily discerned. Life on this planet is very old. Millions upon millions of relatives of whom we have absolutely no recollection or understanding preceded each of us. Almost all of these relatives hunted and fished for a living, lived in huts, tents, and caves, and lived as wanderers, watching innumerable sunrises and sunsets. They knew the seasons and the patterns of the animal life around them. They would be shocked by the way we lead our lives. The tapestry of life is woven in complex patterns into the very fabric of all living things. We are all far more connected to each other than we could possibly ever imagine. The essence of all humanity is set. We are who we are. Our bonds with nature are not easily broken and not to be ignored. We were not made to have cell phones connected to our ears all day, but we have adapted and we have survived. And many of us have prospered. The further evolution of the human species is now both reactive and proactive. We react to the changes in our environment; yet we are forcing unknown changes on ourselves in the form of inoculations of all sorts, antibiotics, organ transplants and—most dramatically and importantly—the deciphering of the human genome and the ultimate changes we may bring upon ourselves as a result of our insatiable curiosity and desire to create the perfect being. In truth, change happens more quickly than we can imagine. I grew up with rotary dial phones, AM radio, and propeller airplanes. Life happens far more quickly than I would like. Every time I blink, I'm five years older. I wish it would slow down.

In reality, we are not such perfect beings as we imagine ourselves. Our need to dominate and conquer is mystifying. Our inhumanity toward ourselves is well documented in the brutal reality of survival of the fittest. Evolutionary biologists tell us that our ultimate battle is to survive against viruses and bacteria that can mutate and adapt in the blink of an eye. Hence, our need to adapt as well.

With all this in mind, we cannot ignore from whence we came. And we cannot ignore the voices that resonate with indecipherable words. I am not foolish enough to suggest that either rustic furniture or rustic settings is the panacea for the world's woes. I am, however, offering that we may just find a bit more comfort and peace in our lives if we occasionally listen to frogs croaking or wolves howling in the night. Maybe if we spent just a bit more time gazing into the heavens or wandering through lush fields, we might find answers to the great questions in our lives. Perhaps if we traveled on the soles of our feet along deserted beaches, we just might come closer to the souls of our very lives. If we connect even occasionally with the calls of nature, we can become better connected to our inner selves and the lives of those who are important to us. Beauty is an end in itself, and the process to get there is life-changing. Beauty comes in all forms. I just happen to love rustic furniture. And a lot of other things as well.

*The ceiling of this sunroom
has been lined with the
bark from birch trees.*

The Art of Rustic

MOST RUSTIC FURNITURE MAKERS lie just outside the mainstream of society. They lead nontraditional lives and are, quite honestly, a bit eccentric. Some build furniture for the money, some enjoy the independent lifestyle, and others just enjoy working with their hands. Most are aspiring craftsmen, and some —just a few—have elevated themselves to the noble distinction of artist. And this is not an easy position to either acquire or maintain. However, the struggle to achieve is a heroic one. We are all born with skills, and one form of heroism is the courage to pursue and develop a latent talent. As individuals, we have the lifelong responsibility of cultivating ourselves. Some individuals, however, are just lucky enough to have been born with talents far beyond those of many people on the planet. When they find the right medium for their expression, magic happens. As a retired teacher, I've been privileged to watch a few individuals blossom once they found the right medium. As a musician, I have spent many years playing scales, learning patterns, and struggling to get my fingers to play the music I hear in my head. Others, only a few, get it instantly—or so it seems.

Rustic accessories fit nicely into the shelves and nooks of a narrow cupboard made by Barney Bellinger. The cupboard's legs are made of yellow birch. An original painting graces its front.

Blending objects into constructed pieces is a specialty of Barney Bellinger.

This most impressive queen-sized bed includes fishing poles, bobbers,

fallow-deer antlers, and stones, as well as a superb original painting.

Every once in a while I get to perform with a young teenager who has been given the gift of music and can play far better than I or my fellow aging musicians. We are not jealous; we're thrilled that another has found his talent and is willing to develop what few of us can only hope to be. We enjoy their music and consider it an honor to be able to play with them. They always make the rest of us sound better. And that's life. It's something we all have to accept. As the old Jedi Knight expression goes, "There's always a bigger fish!"

If I may make a few generalizations about the unusual breed of rustic furniture makers, it's these: Most have little regard for traditional convention. If the fish are biting, they're fishing. Many are shortsighted—in their work they can be incredibly detail-oriented, but unfortunately, deadlines seem to elude them. Few can see the forest through the trees. Most of them have tons of interests. I've had lively conversations with numerous rustic builders on all kinds of esoteric subjects. It's incredibly refreshing to experience the fact that not only can many individuals create great art but they also have the profound capacity to recognize it, understand it, and enjoy it at the same time.

Most rustic artists are talented at lots of things. They are accomplished musicians, chess players, fly fishermen, mechanics, motorcycle fanatics, chefs, or indulgent in other pursuits. They appreciate small things. While gathering wood with Peter Winter one late autumn day, he called me over and we marveled for a considerable time over the beauty of a two-foot tree whose branches were so contorted that the form of the tree was quite extraordinary. Barney Bellinger, with whom I am fishing

Detail of a typical Bellinger painting.

buddies, constantly comments on the quality of light we see in the early mornings and evenings on our fishing trips.

Truly accomplished artists hear other voices that most people don't hear. Drums beat loudly in their heads. These people are absolute perfectionists. Details are monumental but nothing gets overlooked. They lose themselves in their work and time does not exist.

Time means little to these artists. They are almost always late. But I respect and love all of them . . . even the ones I don't get along with! Artists see things differently. They have the ability to interpret things differently. They have the capacity to make the world a better place. However we perceive them or they perceive themselves, the world is a better place because of artists and the pursuit of the artistic.

But the notion of art is not to be lost solely on artists or the megatalented. Art is a form of being. Art is a mode in which to conduct our lives. It is a foundation for the betterment of all humanity. Art is not limited to painting or sculpture; the most humble behaviors (e.g., folding clothes, digging ditches) can easily transform our lives if pursued with beauty in mind. A job well done is art in itself. Its rewards are self-evident. While not new, this is a profound thought and one that should be acculturated into the very fabric of our society. It would be a better world if more of us pursued beauty in all our endeavors.

The Realm of the Artistic

These statements raise all kinds of questions. Is the satisfaction an accomplished rustic artist achieves any different from the satisfaction an absolute beginner achieves when his first piece of rustic furniture is complete, even though it may be, according to the standards of others, less than mediocre? Does society reward or even acknowledge individual effort? Do we place too much emphasis on function and occasionally ignore form for its own sake? Do we spend enough time teaching the qualities of beauty to others? Do we teach others to seek beauty in their lives? Do we fail to realize that truth is one of the highest forms of beauty? Do we teach that our quality of life is vastly improved by the mere appreciation of art?

Art is not what we think. There are no rules in the universe dictating what art is. You won't find art on the atomic charts. There are no physical rules depicting the nature of art. Newton had no laws regarding the existence of art. It is not

The tall clock is the creation of husband-and-wife team Jerry and Jessica Farrell. Jerry is the builder; Jessica painted the bear. An antique hickory chair and replica telephone complete the ambience.

Brian Kelly built this oversized rustic bookcase for a 1920s lodge in the Adirondacks.

predictable; it's not a calculation of two plus two. Art does not exist unless we identify it as such. And if we are not conscious of art and beauty, then art does not exist. So, what happens to an individual when he or she encounters art? At first glance, the pupils tend to dilate, the heartbeat initially quickens and then slows down, the flow of blood initially speeds up, the limbic system—the oldest part of our brain—lights up under PET scans, activity in other areas of the brain tends to localize as our concentration increases. Neural activity increases in the right frontal lobes of the brain. We lose ourselves in the thought of the moment. Art is not a painting or a sculpture. It is a state of mind, a condition of being, a moment of consciousness, and a spike in the electricity of life. Art is a verb, not an adjective. It is a process during which time becomes irrelevant and there is significantly less perception of outside stimuli. We become focused on other things and often forget about ourselves. Life is far more interesting with art in it. The pursuit of beauty allows us to enjoy ourselves. Our constant need for approval from others diminishes when we find passion in our own pursuits. Internal motivation is far more rewarding and relevant then external rewards. Art, trite as it sounds, is a gift from the gods. It is the constant and enduring pursuit for quality, excellence, and perfection in any endeavor. It is the only reason for living.

Mark Catman created these high-end fishing creels from the bark of fallen birch trees. The collection rests on a sofa table by Barney Bellinger that features one of his original rustic scenery paintings. The tabletop is flaming birch.

Rustic Art as Furniture

Simply put, rustic furniture artists incorporate natural elements of organic materials in their forms. Little or no attempt is made to alter, disguise, or disfigure the material used. Often the bark is left on the many branches, roots, limbs, and trunks that are used in the construction. The more disfigured the elements, the better. Burls, knots, and aberrations of all sorts imbue the furniture with character. In spite of this, refinement, comfort, and sophistication tend to be the norm with advanced pieces. These great pieces are well constructed, tight, and have perfect copes and scribes. Their forms seem to have a sensuous flow. Bark, if left on, is tight and not rotten. Rustic furniture is not painted, heavily varnished, or excessively polished. In short, the viewer knows exactly what kind of material was used, whether it is wood, antlers, horns, or other organic materials. For a number of reasons, rustic furniture makers today are significantly more accomplished than they were five years ago. First, many of them have been working diligently to improve their skills. At the same time, talented new crafters have entered the market. Individuals like Chris Wager, who apprenticed with Barney Bellinger, have developed a dramatic new flair in traditional Adirondack furniture. Randy Holden of Skowhegan, Maine, began creating rustic furniture just within the past few years and already builds some of the most organic and original pieces ever seen. His furniture falls into the realm of absolute fantasy art. Along with this, new tools and materials have aided builders in their effort to make pieces of the highest possible quality.

Randy Holden has a reputation for innovative design, as evidenced by this two-door, five-drawer sideboard.

An Adirondack tall chest by Chris Wager features drawer pulls made of roots and branches from yellow birch trees. The drawers are constructed with dovetail joinery.

Tom and Bill Welsh constructed a leather-top coffee table with an ornate apron and legs made from deer antlers. The author designed the hickory entertainment center. The hickory tall-case clock was made in Indiana around 1910. Floral arrangement by Michele Kylloe.

The Evolution of Rustic Furniture Making

Today we are in the third period of American rustic furniture. The first period began in the mid-1800s and lasted until the early 1900s. During that time, rustic builders in the Adirondacks (usually guides and/or caretakers) initiated, based on designs originating in Europe and the Orient many years earlier, what would become known as Adirondack furniture. Pieces in this genre typically were covered with birch bark or heavily adorned with intricate twig patterns known as mosaic. Adirondack items were also made of both bark-on and bark-off cedar. At the same time, gypsies, Amish, and other groups of itinerants in the South and Midwest also initiated unique, regionally distinctive forms of rustic furniture.

Beginning in the early 1890s, builders in Indiana began creating a unique style of rustic furniture that was to become

known as Indiana Hickory. Established in Indiana because of the vast stands of hickory trees—which provided the hardest and strongest wood in North America—the Old Hickory Chair Company was the first of at least ten different companies that would sell hickory furniture worldwide and have a continuing and profound impact on rustic style in America. It is still part of the rustic fabric in high-end resorts, lodges, and residences all across the country.

Accessories make the room: the ornate sideboard was made by Chris Wager. The wall mirror is an antique from Switzerland, circa the 1890s. The table lamps with stained-glass shades are the creations of John Bennett.

This dining room set was built in the 1930s. The massive stone fire-place provides a stately ambience for this most impressive setting.

Girded with the owner's books and family photos, this living room was constructed in Adirondack Park in the 1930s. An original Tiffany table lamp rests on an ornate cherry-top table by Peter Winter. Taxidermy of all sorts is thematic throughout the home. The piano is a source of entertainment, especially on long winter nights.

The second period began in the 1930s, around the time that Thomas Molesworth opened a small furniture shop in Cody, Wyoming. His furnishings incorporated indigenous Rocky Mountain materials such as lodgepole pine and antlers, along with traditional western motifs such as Indian and cowboy designs. Molesworth furniture, later to become known as cowboy or western, was the quintessential dude-ranch style but was sold worldwide. Molesworth spawned an extended cottage industry, as many builders throughout the Rocky Mountains were influenced by his creations.

The 1930s also saw a rebirth of builders working in the Adirondacks, including Lee Fountain, who produced large quantities of rockers and stump-based tables from yellow birch trees. A large commercial firm in Lake Placid also produced traditional birch-bark furniture in the Adirondack style. The decade also saw the introduction of three more firms in Indiana that were building hickory furniture.

*A bureau and root mirror bene-
fited from Jerry Farrell's attention to detail and impressive
workmanship. The paintings
adorning the drawer fronts are
by Jessica Farrell.*

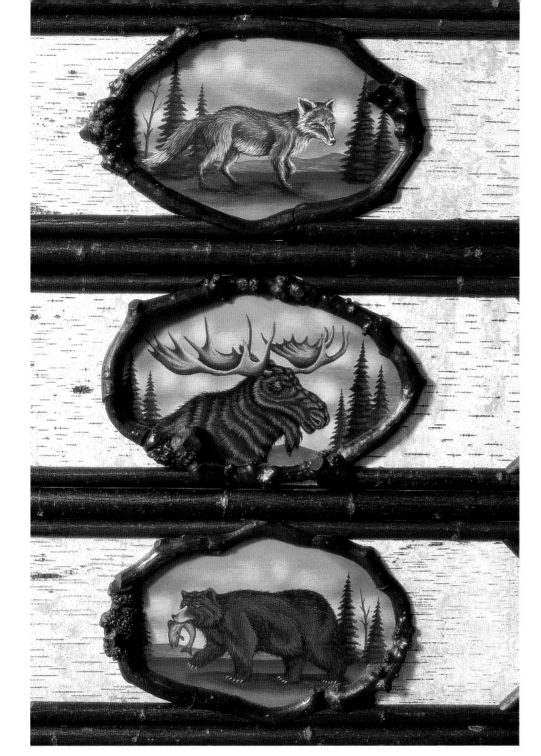

Detail of paintings by Jessica Farrell.

In the 1980s, due to resurgence of interest in rustic furniture and rustic living, the third period of rustic furniture evolved. The Old Hickory Furniture Company reopened its doors after a twenty-year hiatus. Within a few years, at least four other firms around the country began building rustic hickory furniture as well, and several builders in the Adirondacks, including Ken Heitz and Jerry Farrell, began building quality rustic furniture. Today, numerous artisans living in and around the Adirondack Park are building rustic furniture for a living. About that time, significant interest in antique rustic furniture began in earnest, and collectors began amassing impressive collections of high-end rustic furniture, driving up auction prices to new records. Simultaneously, several builders in the Cody, Wyoming, area—including

Mike Patrick, Lester Santos, Jimmy Covert, and others—began building traditional furniture inspired by Molesworth's designs. A plethora of builders around the country have begun manufacturing high-quality furnishings, including chandeliers, upholstered pieces, case goods, and other items, from the antlers of elk, moose, fallow deer, and red stag. Amish and gypsy chairs have become popular again and numerous builders around the country are thriving because of this interest. Finally, builders on the West Coast—Matt Madsen, Phil Clausen, Brent McGregor—began utilizing indigenous materials such as redwood, myrtle, manzanita, and juniper to create a very distinctive West Coast style of rustic furniture.

This tall entertainment center by rustic builder Lester Santos, of Cody, Wyoming, is enhanced by original paintings on the front by George Dabich, also of Cody. The doors and drawers are trimmed in leather.

Above: Front view of a tall cupboard by award-winning artist Jimmy Covert, of Cody, Wyoming. Covert has long been recognized for his impressive creativity, superb designs and outstanding construction detailing.

Left: Side view of the tall cupboard shows Covert's creative blending of walnut and juniper.

Why Choose Rustic?

But why the resurgent interest in rustic? And why now? The back-to-nature movement certainly has had an influence. Beginning in the early 1970s, interest in the environment and environmental causes came to the fore. A new consciousness developed in response to environmental issues such as damage from DDT, air pollution, strip mines, deforestation, ozone depletion, and water quality.

But the real kick-start for the third phase of rustic popularity would have to be lifestyle. Endless hours of mindless television viewing, long commutes to and from work, plastic-covered white sofas, tubular furniture, computers, video games, and on and on began to drain the human spirit. By losing connection with the natural world, we began to lose connection with ourselves, and our souls began to wander in unhealthy directions.

Deep inside us, we craved something more. Log cabins, lakeside living, vacations to wilderness areas, fireplaces, wildlife, walks in the woods, sunsets, camping, and . . . rustic furniture. Furniture styled in the rustic fashion is simple and honest. It does not lie to us. Its textured surfaces feel good to the touch. It speaks deeply to us. It's fun and full of humor. It's carefree and it looks us right in the face and tells us to take our shoes off and relax. Don't take things so seriously, it says.

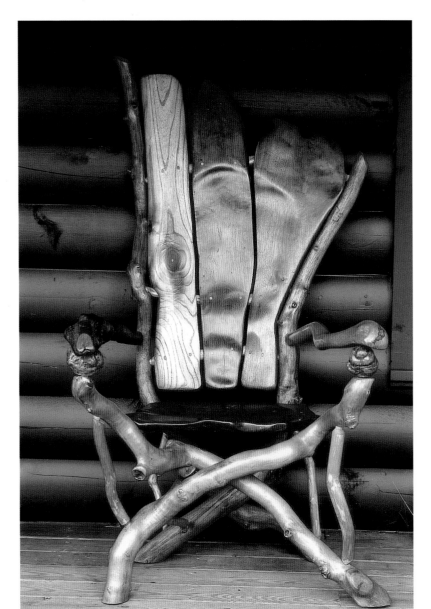

Life is too short. It's a necessity in our lives that we take it easy once in a while. We need to escape wars, terrorist attacks, bombings, plane crashes, anthrax, Ebola, and AIDS. This is not to suggest that we should ignore the complexities of our modern lives, but we really do need to relax once in a while. Rustic furniture and rustic living can help us do that.

Mike Emelianoff worked a masterful blend of American beech, black oak, black cherry, English walnut, and pelonia in this armchair. Panel-back chairs such as this are a mainstay of rustic builders around the country.

Adirondack legend Jack Leadley built these impressive rocking chairs.

The woven material on the seats, arms, and backs is black ash.

This classic western club chair, ottoman, and side chair by Lester Santos would present well in an elegant setting even though the theme is rustic.

Realistically, we convince ourselves that the more structure and discipline we are able to incorporate into our lives, the more successful, in general, we become. For instance, the more that lawyers, accountants, mathematicians, researchers of all sorts, etc., stay within the parameters ascribed to them, the more successful they become at their jobs and in their lives. Most of us lead incredibly structured and disciplined lives. We seem to fill every last second of our waking hours with disciplines that we deem necessary for our own satisfaction and happiness. And we are all subject to time clocks, mortgage payments, schedules, tax dates, holiday stress, and deadlines of all sorts. On the other hand, nature abounds with freedom.

Branches, roots, trees, and organic structures of all kinds grow (within reason) wherever they want. Birds often fly just because they want to. Otters and seals play just for the fun of it. Their freedom knows few bounds. It is that freedom that we so envy and need in our own lives.

Rustic furniture embodies all the freedom of nature in its numerous structures and designs. That freedom is one notion why rustic furniture has become so popular today. Rustic living represents the significant amount of freedom that each of us has given up in order to function within today's high-tech world.

Original chair and desk by Lester Santos.

A forest green–painted floor provides a solid ground for geometric banisters, a birch swing, an umbrella stand, and armchairs on a traditional Adirondack porch.

Rustic Art for the Home

We can enjoy the freedom that rustic living offers by incorporating rustic furniture and décor into our homes. Whether relaxing in an Adirondack chair on the porch or entertaining friends in a casual kitchen, it is possible for all of us to escape from our busy lives for a while and embrace nature through rustic living.

Nothing about a home's exterior gives more pleasure and comfort than a porch—and the bigger, the better. They were on every house up until the Victorian period, when some half-baked architect invented apartment buildings—and there went one of the principal places for socialization in western society. Wraparound porches are best, but any porch will work. Porches need comfortable rockers and other things on which to sit. They shoud include areas where both people and pets can lie down and take a nap. A table and chairs seem almost necessities—nothing fancy, but a place for the kids to play board games, and sooner or later someone will need a place to repair an old outboard motor or rearrange a tackle box.

Other furnishings possibilities for the porch are a lift-top box to put things in and a porch swing of modest range (for safety reasons). Porches also need textiles such as old-looking blankets and pillows—after all, one can never have enough pillows.

This antique tall-back hickory rocker rests on the author's front porch along with colorful antique textiles.

A pair of upholstered club chairs provide the homeowners a place for relaxation in front of this fireplace. The mantel was created from a heavily burled lodgepole pine.

The living room is usually the first room we see when entering a home. This is where we spend much of our waking hours and where we often entertain our guests. We this area to make a statement of both comfort and impressiveness. Some people choose to have their living rooms look like museums—look but don't touch anything. Others prefer the lived-in look where casual rules. Rustic living rooms are usually the latter.

In a rustic living room, attention to lighting and color is important. Light should be soft. Colors should blend, but not too much. Red is a good accent color to jump-start your living room. They also need to have intimate settings, and they should be inviting and capable of fostering relationships. Chairs and couches should not be so far apart that you have to use binoculars to see your guests. Pets in rustic settings should be allowed to sleep anywhere they want. Flowers and dried plants remind us of the outdoors and should be used liberally around the house. Collections of rustic things should be prominently displayed.

An impressive array of Adirondack collectibles—including colorful antique baskets, snowshoes, and textiles—is on display in a small living room. The hickory settee was made in Indiana.

Hickory chairs fit stunningly in a dining room alcove.

Dining rooms are perhaps the most fun rooms in the house. Here we fulfill some of our most basic needs, get closer to our friends, and, perhaps, consume more then we should. We should always give thanks for our blessings in this room. We should never fret if we spill something on the table, and the chairs should always be comfortable. Remember to not hang your chandelier too low over the dining room table, as the bright light may interfere with the ability to see your guests across the table. Avoid bark edges on dining room tabletops—our forearms are sensitive to rough textures, and slivers could be a hazard. Be aware of the heights of arms on the chairs; if the arms are too high, chairs will not slide under the dining table and you'll sit uncomfortably far from your dinner.

This colorful, fun dining room rests in a beautiful 1930s
Adirondack lakeside home. Both antique and contemporary
rustic furnishings and accessories are comfortable in the setting.

*Contemporary leather
chairs blend naturally
with the rustic furnishings
in this log home setting.*

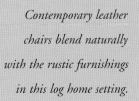

Bedroom setting from the Ralph Kylloe Gallery. The queen-sized bed was made from kiln-dried yellow birch trees. Colorful rustic textiles accent the setting.

Innate organic forms are used to advantage on this bed frame.

Far left: Butternut tops this combination bureau and matching mirror by Brian Kelly.

Bedrooms are the most intimate rooms in the house. We need to feel completely secure in these rooms. Everything in this room should be functional and there should be lots of space to put our stuff. Rustic beds should always bring a smile to our faces. Beds should be tight and solid. They should not creak and groan every time we turn over. You can never have enough mirrors in either bedrooms or bathrooms. Bedrooms should also have numerous places to throw our clothes and put on our shoes.

Kids' bedrooms need to be fun. Single beds are perfect, as kids need room to play and spread out all their stuff. Significant wall space is necessary for hanging posters of rock stars and NASCARs. Don't even think of keeping the kids' rooms clean. It's a losing battle. Perpetually messy rooms are not to be taken as personal insults to parents. Have lots of family and friends' photos in bedrooms. They keep us company and remind us of loved ones and good times.

What queen wouldn't enjoy relaxing on this bed in a house overlooking a stellar Adirondack lake? Chris Wager is the artisan.

This commodious study is the occasional workstation of an international businessman who spends

time in the Adirondacks. The library tabletop is curly maple. The chairs are hickory.

Studies have to be functional. A huge desk and bookshelves everywhere are the key furniture items here. This room should have a sense of humor and fun; you'll get a lot more work done if the room does not appear too serious. Put in extra electrical outlets and phone lines for computers, printers, phones, fax machines, and CD players. Plenty of light is necessary for this room. Above all, remember to have a comfortable easy chair in this room in addition to a desk and chair. And always wear old shoes—when our feet are comfortable we make better decisions.

Bathrooms are humorous as well—how else could we bear to look at ourselves in the buff? Vanities in rustic bathrooms are often made of old barn wood and other organic materials. Before you use these woods, make certain they are absolutely dry and bug-free. Thick slabs of pine make good countertops. These also need to be absolutely dry, about 6 percent

The rich walnut desk, a creation of John Gallis, presently resides in an impressive home outside of Jackson, Wyoming.

Fossil stone countertops couldn't be more appropriate for a rustic kitchen. Fish, insects, and a variety of plants can be seen throughout. Heavy iron is the homeowners' cookware of choice.

An ornate banister extends across the upstairs, drawing one's eye to the height of the open space.

A pair of Spanish-influenced armchairs rests beneath the handrails of the staircase. A cowhide covers the floor.

moisture, or they will split years down the road. Most importantly, the top, sides, and bottom of the slabs need to be treated with spar varnish in order to prevent moisture from entering the wood. Make certain that the bathroom is well ventilated to keep moisture at low levels. Plenty of drawers are needed to hide all our bathroom stuff. Hooks are more functional than towel bars. Think casual.

Kitchens can be the most creative rooms in the entire house. We spend more time in them than we probably realize. Make sure that more than one person can move about comfortably in there at any given time. Popular items for kitchens today are heavy-duty industrial ranges and refrigerators. Utilize this room in the name of art and always remember that Julia Child once said, "Don't make a pig out of yourself!"

Don't forget to name your house. Think of a great camp name like "Camp I Hate My Job" or "Camp Leave Me Alone." A great camp name will give you peace of mind and remind you of better times. Have a sign made and place it prominently on your house so everyone knows your place.

*Unusual bends of a yellow birch tree plus applied white birch bark were the materials that Zen
Baudoux used to craft this unique bar for a contemporary home in the Adirondacks.*

A collection of antique fishing creels is comfy in a narrow bookcase constructed by Brian Kelly of vintage barn boards. The mirror is by Peter Winter.

Colorful textiles dress up a hickory bed for an interesting focal point.

Left: Retractable pocket doors are a fine feature of this grand entertainment center by Brian Kelly. The interior has drawers, adjustable shelves, and a rotating TV tray.

Right: An intricate geometric mosaic is the focal point of this bureau by Chris Wager. The table lamp is by John Bennett. The floral arrangement was created by Michele Kylloe.

This tall western-themed entertainment center is the creation of Lester Santos.

Opposite: George Jacques built this hall table that presently houses the owner's collection of bronzes. The tabletop is maple and the base was created from the stump of a yellow birch tree.

This unique stump-based table with attached stained-glass lamp was made by John Bennett. The wall clock is a Jerry Farrell original.

*An early Barney Bellinger bed, which resides in a beautiful lakeside home in
the northern Adirondacks, is complemented with original floral paintings.*

A crest of fallow-deer antlers crowns a large cupboard, which is filled with a variety of rustic collectibles, including leather-bound books, a stoneware place setting, and creels.

Above: A diminutive Adirondack corner cupboard and root stand are the work of Chris Wager.

Above left: Detail of an armchair by Lester Santos. Lower left: Six-drawer chest by Chris Wager.

Left: Six-drawer birch bark chest by Chris Wager.

Bark-off cedar railings, Adirondack chairs, and colorful container gardens complete this porch in traditional rustic style.

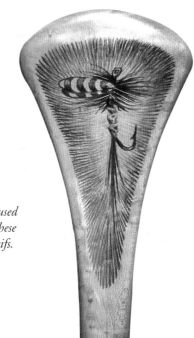

Artist Gary Casagrain used pen and ink to adorn these paddles with rustic motifs.

*Barney Bellinger created this gorgeous stump-
based stand. The painting on the stand is a
floral motif. The floral arrangement in the
antique Adirondack pack basket is by
Michele Kylloe.*

This extraordinary cupboard by Randy Holden demonstrates why he is well known for his nontraditional, nonconformist forms.

Facing: Antique stoves, either coal or wood burning, are quite popular and add both warmth and nostalgia. The antique hickory rocker was made in the 1930s by the Bedford Hickory Furniture Company of Indiana.

A superb collection of antique accessories fills the shelves of this Adirondack birch bark and twig-mosaic cupboard.

Little Lindsey Kylloe adores her "Adirondack George" bedroom, including antique hickory furniture and whimsical bird accessories.

High-end rustic accessories give a contemporary condominium personality.

Veronica Nemethy not only paints the scenes but creates the frames as well. Her rustic art style is augmented by found objects such as birch bark, acorns, pinecones, fungi, twigs, and stones. All the paints and frames are Nemethy originals.

Three works of art by Randy Holden: a unique table, a whimsical floor lamp, and a freestanding hall mirror. The table top and bases are burls from an ancient yellow birch tree. The mirror is made of bark-off cedar.

A trio of rustic artists made this setting possible. The large hall mirror is by Lori Toledo. The shelf was made by Jon Bennett. The dramatic console table by Chris Wager is ornamented with an intricate twig mosaic top and a combination antler and root base.

Opposite: An elaborate entertainment center by Brian Kelly boasts pocket doors that slide to expose a large-screen TV.

Opposite, below left: A mushroom lamp is the signature work of artisan Phil Clausen.

Opposite, below right: Randy Holden made the wonderful floor lamp from a yellow birch stump.

Below: Unique in size, form, and construction, this cupboard brings rustic furniture to a new height. The hinges are completely hand made from roots and twigs. The drawers are lined with designer wallpaper and the mirror is beveled. The top surface is lace wood. The entire composition was envisioned and created by Randy Holden.

An intricate staircase is a focal point of this modern home. The railings, newel posts, and spindles were created from bark-off cedar.

Left: A wildly organic chair by master builder Matt Madsen. The seat and back are of manzanita wood; the rocker arms and legs are twisted juniper.

Right: Juniper provides the organic theme that Lester Santos brought to life in this wonderful chair, complete with hand-tooled and painted leather seat and back.

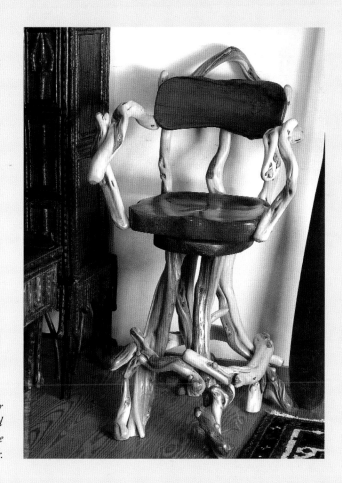

Left: A rocking chair by Matt Madsen is in the California free-form style. The seat back and arms are redwood branches and burls; the rocker legs are twisted juniper.

Right: The bar stool is another Madsen original, with seat and back from redwood burls. The arms and legs are twisted juniper.

Referred to as the 1912 Swedish Homestead, this building is part of the Double D Homestead in the wilds of Montana. The building was dismantled and completely reconstructed by the creative folks at Yellowstone Traditions on the homestead of interior designer Diana Beattie.

Kamp Kylloe

I HAD LOOKED FOR A SMALL CABIN on the shores of Lake George, New York, for six years. But with small lots starting at a half million dollars, my chances of finding and owning something affordable were not good. Nonetheless, one Saturday morning in October a friend called and mentioned that an elderly acquaintance of his was selling a small house and asked if I was interested. ✦ Within the hour my wife and I stood in the doorway of what could only be called a "teardown." It had been unoccupied for six years. The plumbing and septic systems were gone. All the electrical wiring needed to be replaced, and the roof had several inches of mold growing on it. There were no screens, insulation, or foundation, but it did have a view of the lake, a great beach, a deepwater boat dock, and a mooring for a sailboat! ✦ I looked at my wife and then back at the owner. "I'll take it," I said. My wife rolled her eyes in disbelief as I wrote out the check. In truth, I should have taken a match to the house.

Purchased in the late fall by the author, the camp had been unoccupied for six years. It was not insulated and needed new wiring, a septic system, roof, insulation, and plumbing.

The interior of the cabin had badly worn carpet and came complete with beehives, mice, and used furniture in various states of disrepair.

Ultimately the roofline was redesigned, large picture windows were installed, and the entire building was covered with bark-on hemlock.

But I had other plans. The following day my contractor said that he and his crew would be able to start within the week, and I looked forward to Thanksgiving on the shores of the finest lake in North America. Unfortunately, I was to feel the full brunt of the 50 percent rule: in essence, all construction takes 50 percent longer than the contractor tells you it will and costs 50 percent more than what you were told would be the final cost of a "complete makeover." The project was not complete until the following spring and cost significantly more than the agreed-on price. A review of the local regulations revealed that I was allowed to build only on the exact footprint of the existing house, which was 808 square

feet on the ground. The house could be no more than nineteen and a half feet tall. It would be a very small but comfortable four-season vacation house when completed. Considering that I showed up on the job site a week after construction started and all that was standing were three walls of ancient two-by-fours on cinder bricks, I should have followed my first instinct and burned the place to the ground. I could have built a wonderful small log cabin—and if I had to do it over, that's what I would have done. The contractor for the home, Pinky O'Dell, was instrumental in solving many design problems while keeping the house both rustic in nature and aesthetic in appeal. It wouldn't be what it is without him. We persisted and used as much of the old material as possible. Even so, by the time the project was completed, the costs of rehabbing the place were identical to the price of building a new building.

We used the old windows when possible and added two large picture windows to bring in extra light. We were careful not to disturb the roots of the huge, 150-year-old white pine trees that surrounded the building when we rebuilt the

Opposite: The interior of the cabin was ideally suited for an ever-growing collection of antique camp signs, canoe paddles, fishing creels, Adirondack pack baskets, and other related cabin accessories. A 1930s kayak and a red-stag antler chandelier hang from the ceiling.

The kitchen island was covered with bark-on hemlock. The island top and kitchen countertop were covered with three-inch-thick slabs of white pine. The floors are southern yellow pine.

The small living room contains hickory furniture designed by the author. Damaged Indian rugs were cut up and made into colorful throw pillows. Taxidermy and rustic accessories complete the room.

septic system. Unfortunately, the water table was very high, so a leach field could not be added and we wound up putting in a holding tank that has to be pumped out every two years. We also had to anchor down the tank because, we were told, as the water table rises and sinks, holding tanks in the neighborhood occasionally float up and break through the ground. We added a new roof high enough to include a comfortable sleeping loft. We covered the exterior of the building with bark-on hemlock. Hemlock is a highly textured wood that blends perfectly with the indigenous mature white pine trees. No covering or stain (varnish or lacquer) was used to seal the siding. We added a deck with a railing made of bark-on

A small back bedroom is outfitted with a custom-made yellow birch bed covered with antique camp blankets. Old camp signs and creels add a sense of fun to the room.

cedar, which the local squirrels stripped clean within a few weeks to use for nesting material. The interior was to house a very extensive and growing collection of antique rustic accessories, including snowshoes, camp signs, taxidermy, fishing memorabilia, canoe paddles, and other goodies. I designed most of the furnishings and we had them built in our own workshops. The entire project turned out quite nicely and is the joy of my three-year-old daughter and her friends. In our bathroom hangs a sign that says, "You never realize how many friends you have until you own a lake house!" Weekends at Kamp Kylloe get booked up a year in advance. If you want to visit, make your reservations early!

The curtains in another small bedroom were fashioned from a red-and-black hunter pattern available at many outdoor stores. The curtain rods are two-inch-thick yellow birch poles. Deer antlers hold the rod aloft.

The mirror, covered with pinecones, fungus, birch bark, and twigs, was made by rustic artist Lori Toledo. The small antique pillows are souvenir collectibles stuffed with aromatic cedar.

This bedroom offers a peeled-cedar bed and paint-by-numbers rustic duck scenes. A collection of high-end snowshoes lines the upper walls.

Chris Wager designed and constructed this sideboard in traditional
Adirondack style. Antique photos and related accessories complete the setting.

A small back room became an office. Canoe paddles
and birch bark bookcases complete the office setting.

The birch bark cupboard was constructed by Chris Wager. A moose head guards the entranceway to a small bunkroom, a back bedroom, and a sleeping loft.

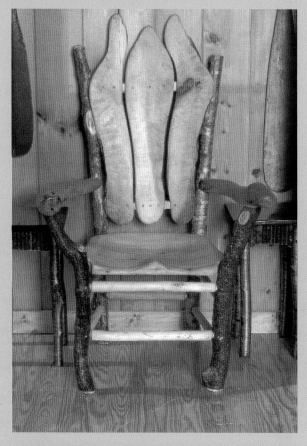

Top left: Tom Welsh constructed this massive armchair. Tom uses solid, hand-carved wood for the seats and local dried hardwoods such as yellow birch and maple for the arms, legs, and back. Lower left: A built-in box shelf serves as a display case for part of the author's extensive collection of antique birch bark picture frames. Above: A corner of the living room shows off more of the ever-growing and -changing collection.

A side view of a birch bark cupboard, massive armchair, and moose head. Colorful baskets and paddles add life to any room.

Avalanche Ranch

NESTLED IN THE ROCKY MOUNTAINS of Idaho is a narrow valley replete with moose, deer, willow trees, trout streams, and avalanche debris. Here lies Avalanche Ranch, occupying a calm corner of the area. The ungulates and ducks take their time about moving for a mere vehicle. Constructed in the mid-sixties, the ranch has recently been refurbished by interior designer Lisa Butterbrodt, who both commissioned and found a large gathering of handcrafted furniture items. Through the remodeling, the home has acquired a significant and profoundly comfortable appeal.

Nestled off the main road, the Avalanche Ranch appears unassuming at first glance. It consists of a main house—made of locally cut logs—a bunkhouse, a horse barn, and a prodigious trout pond.

This elaborate front door was custom-made of dried lodgepole pine by local artist Randy Edgar.

Handmade hardware gives this mosaic front door further distinction.

For this highly ornate fireplace, Randy Edgar turned raw materials into an artistic mantel, blending the colors to match other logs used throughout the house. The lodgepole burls of the mantel were scouted from high elevations on horseback.

Naturally shed antlers are commonly used to make a wide variety of furnishings throughout the West. These kitchen bar stools with elk-antler backrests were made by Ron Shanor.

Decorator and craftsman Doug Tedrow of Wood River Rustics helped create a rustic atmosphere in the kitchen. He made the cabinets and covered the countertops with copper. The floor is hand painted with classic American Indian motifs.

Virtually a gallery of rustic artistry, this setting boasts an armchair and ottoman made from lodgepole pine by Doug Tedrow. The cushions are covered with buffalo hide, and a Tedrow original cabinet looms in the background. The table lamp on the small cabinet was created by Cloudbird.

This burled lodgepole staircase was fashioned by Randy
Edgar. The classic Adirondack cabinet in the background
was created by Barney Bellinger of Sampson Bog Studio.
Lined with birch bark and adorned with hardwood twigs,
such cabinets are ideal as storage places, servers, and display
cases for collectibles of all kinds.

This large entertainment center was made by Doug Tedrow.
Working in the style of Reverend Ben Davis, whose early 1900s
work included the application of chip-carved twigs, Tedrow has
produced numerous spectacular pieces for many of the great
ranches and lodges in the West.

Opposite:
Surrounded by
antique Indian rugs
from the region of
Ganado, Arizona,
this lodgepole bed by
Glenn Burleigh fea-
tures a layered, soft-
leather bedspread.

This cabinet, made
by Doug Tedrow
from locally cut
pine branches, was
commissioned for
Avalanche Ranch.

This classical western bed, built in
Colorado, is complete with pillows
and textiles in Indian motif.

A pronghorn antelope guards this guest bedroom containing twin beds likely made from cottonwood trees. The chandelier was made in cowboy fashion, including several pairs of horseshoes.

Willow shoots were the medium for this small bedside table by Thome George. Light, airy and often whimsical furnishings by Thome are collectors' delights for both traditional and nontraditional settings.

The leather curtains and pillows throughout the house were made by Linda Shore Perez. The curtains shown here serve as a door for the powder room.

Antlers serve as attractive accents in this bathroom, as seen on the mirror and on the handcrafted bathroom vanity by Doug Tedrow.

Design influences from around the world blend effortlessly with the rustic style. Here, curtains made from colorful Mexican textiles add life to the room.

This L-shaped bureau and table lamp were hand-made by rustic artist Ron Shanor of Cody, Wyoming.

This entertainment center by Ron Shanor offers a rustic symmetry with clean lines.

This lodgepole chandelier, with lights nestled among the burls and twists of the wood, was created by Ron Shanor.

Copper basins are the perfect highlight for this vanity by Doug Tedrow. A section of elk antler serves as a toilet-paper holder.

Drawer pulls and handles in this bathroom are crafted of leather and silver
in a western motif. The countertops are
made of chestnut.

Window treatments in many of the rooms
were made from soft leather by Linda
Shore Perez. This drapery is accented with
Indian beading along the top.

The chandelier of hand-forged metal features animals in a forest.

The western ambiance of this home is enhanced by a lively decorative style using antique chaps and taxidermy hung on the staircase walls.

A fisherman's mirror crafted by Barney Bellinger hangs in the hallway.

The backyard deck has a glorious overlook of the mountains and is complete with rustic cedar furniture from Romancing the Woods. The pond to the rear of the deck houses a school of huge rainbow trout for ranch guests who enjoy watching or fishing.

*In this cozy bunkhouse at Avalanche Ranch, which once
served as the horse stable, the interior walls are lined with
both log and rough-cut wavy board siding.*

A cedar gazebo by Romancing the Woods provides shelter for a private tête-à-tête. Hilary Heminway designed and refurbished the antique chuck wagon.

A chuckwagon interior designed by Hilary
Heminway invites visitors to recline under a secreting
canopy on benches overflowing with pillows.

Log Haven

LOCATED ON THE SLOPES of a world-class ski resort in the White Mountains of New Hampshire, this comfortable home is called Log Haven. Designed by architect Bob Cogan, one needs to drive slowly when approaching the area as to avoid any number of moose in the immediate vicinity. Finishing touches for the home were added by interior designer Barbara Collum. ❦ Both modern and rustic in perspective, a few of the things that make this home so comfortable are the inclusion of birch bark as wallpaper in several of the rooms, and the use of very functional furnishings that the kids take delight in using.

A view of the living room from the balcony. Classic contemporary rustic fabrics, inspired by traditional Native American patterns, cover the upholstered furniture. The floors and interior walls are covered with wide knotty-pine boards.

A game room includes a bar covered with birch bark. The bar and matching bar stool were made by Ron Nobbs of Rangely, Maine. Rustic mirrors and camp signs complete the look.

MAINE GUIDE
SERVICE

Rustic artist Randy Holden made this chandelier of yellow birch. The shades are lined with thin strips of birch bark.

A ground-floor view of the living room shows the floor-to-ceiling fireplace adorned with a moose head and a classic rustic painting. A moose-antler chandelier illuminates the room. Randy Holden made the yellow birch floor lamp in the foreground. A variety of rustic accessories, including Adirondack pack baskets, picture frames, creels and other items, complete the room.

On the second floor of
the home is a child's
room. These twin beds
were made from yellow
birch trees and are
enhanced by a 1930s
patchwork quilt.

The walls of this second-floor bathroom are completely lined with bark from birch trees.

Unlike many other entertainment centers, this one is complete with a swinging TV tray. Its shelves adjust to accommodate numerous electronic gadgets. It was made by Ron Nobbs.

The walls of this second bathroom are also covered with birch bark.

Rocky Mountain Lodge

HIDDEN IN A SECLUDED REGION of the northern Rocky Mountains resides this extraordinary home, referred to by the owner simply as The Lodge. Designed by architect Brooks Pittman, the owner hired interior designer Heidi Weiskopf to complete the setting. Decorated as a man's home, it celebrates the owner's passion for hunting, fishing, golf, and entertaining. The numerous features join together to create a comfortable, inviting residence. Equally as important as the interior are the views afforded by the setting. Moose and elk are everywhere and an occasional grizzly or black bear add a thrill to the complete experience of the home. World-class fly fishing and challenging downhill and cross-country skiing are only minutes away. Built to withstand massive snow loads, the home endures as a monument of innovative style and comfort.

Nestled on a ridge overlooking a stunning terrain of valleys and mountains, this home sits in the land of grizzly bears, elk, moose, and mule deer.

The entryway is hung with four different ram's heads. An armchair and matching ottoman in the foreground were made by Tim Groth. The innovative architecture includes the use of slab boards on several interior walls.

The living room of this home includes rustic artwork, hand-made rustic chairs, and upholstered items designed for comfort.

Tim Groth created these dining room chairs and covered the seats with green leather. The massive dining room table was created from lodgepole pine. Groth also built the bar stools.

A nature theme permeates the bathroom. An inverted branch serves as
an interesting base for the stone basin and soap dish. The mirror frame
is a hollowed-out slab of maple. The wallpaper features birch trees.

An impala guards the
rustic staircase leading
to the game room.

Below: The huge upstairs den was created for entertaining. Outfitted
with a large wet bar and regulation-size pool table, the room also
contains numerous of the owner's taxidermy trophy mounts.

Leftover branches and slab material were cleverly incorporated into the structural beams to create this interesting setting in a small bar area of the main entertainment room.

Diana Beattie Guest Camp

DIANA BEATTIE, OF DIANA BEATTIE INTERIORS, is one of the most accomplished interior designers working today. I featured her Montana home in my last book, *Rustic Artistry for the Home.* So when she called and said that she had just completed a small guest home on her Montana ranch, I knew that it was a place to be seen. Renovated by the log-cabin wizards at Yellowstone Traditions in conjunction with architect Ann Miller, the house is a marvel of innovation and rustic comfort. Originally built in 1912 by a Swedish carpenter, the home was found just north of Bozeman, Montana. After purchase, it was dismantled by rustic woodworker David Laitinen and reassembled on a mountain wilderness slope in the northern Rocky Mountains. Although I had spent many nights at the Beattie Ranch, I got lost on my return trip. Snow had just fallen and cows and moose on the gravel road required that we drive slowly. Fortunately a caretaker was looking for us and politely drove us to the house as the sun quickly set. As with my many other visits to Diana's estate, the coyotes welcomed us with frequent howls in the background. At the house we found that the fires had been laid and were ready to be lit; gourmet refreshments awaited consumption. Diana's taste for traditional Scandinavian, and specifically Swedish, influences sets her style apart. She is one of just a few people who have incorporated this style into rustic settings.

Local rustic artist David Laitinen made the front door and other furniture throughout the house. David's specialty is recycled wood.

The Swedish folk motif on the inside front door was painted in classical Scandinavian colors.

The living room of the Beattie guest house is
complete with warm rustic colors, Scandinavian-
influenced furniture, rustic accessories, and
floral arrangements. The stones for the fireplace
were dug from the ground surrounding the house.

Kitchen cabinets made of old barn boards by the creative folks
at Yellowstone Traditions intensify the rustic flavor of this home.
The refrigerator, countertops, and sink are lined with copper.

The Beattie breakfast nook contains an antique Old Hickory table, country painted chairs, a tall-case Scandinavian clock, and floral arrangements.

The downstairs bedroom is cozy with a roaring
fireplace and painted crib beds made by David
Laitinen. Artist Jennifer Bessen hand-stenciled
the walls and painted the framed art.

The upstairs bedroom contains an antique four-poster bed covered with a 1930s American crazy quilt.

An early, original blue-painted cupboard, rustic accessories, and roots and branches used as décor add a sense of warmth and comfort to the living room.

A vintage shed added to the property houses bunk beds and
other kids' furniture. The exterior is hung with old tools and
an assortment of memorabilia often associated with the West.

Lake George Boathouse

NESTLED ON THE SHORES OF A LAKE where crystal-clear water allows for visibility to depths of about twenty feet, an Adirondacks boathouse apartment is a statement of both form and efficiency.  Underneath the house, there is indoor space for two boats, and it also has an upstairs apartment and a large deck. The exterior of the home has been sided with shake shingles. The railings, made of peeled cedar are arranged in geometric patterns. Inside, the floors, wall, and ceiling are wood. Futons are rolled out in the evenings for sleeping. Designed by architect Michael Bird.

Although small in size, this combination boathouse/upstairs

apartment offers great style and comfort to the owner's family.

There is space for two boats, an upstairs apartment, and a large deck. The exterior of the home has been sided with shake shingles. The railings, made of peeled cedar, are arranged in geometric patterns.

The interior floors, wall, and ceiling are wood.

Futons are rolled out in the evenings for sleeping.

Left: The blanket chest, which opens from the top, presently provides resting space for a replica of a 1950s mahogany motorboat. Brian Kelly made the blanket chest.

Right: The apartment maintains many different angles, which makes the house appear larger than it really is. The kitchen island countertop is Corian. The bar stools are made of hickory.

The flooring of the deck is made of pressure-treated lumber.

Roddy Lodge/Elk Run

A FEW MILES NORTH OF YELLOWSTONE NATIONAL PARK, in the Rocky Mountains of Montana, lies a region where the elk, moose, bears, and deer wander aimlessly in the backyard. It's a place where the monstrous trout in the Gallatin River hit on every cast of a dry fly and where the views and colors are so spectacular that one has to pause for a moment to remind oneself that the setting is actually real. 🌲 Enamored by the 1930s designs of Lewis Hill, who completed many of the extraordinary rustic structures in Glacier National Park, the owners of this home sought to both replicate and capture the spirit often found in the buildings that grace our national parks. During a recent extended winter, the contractor and architect Larry Pearson of Bozeman, Montana, were forced to ski an enormous area of ground to find just the right site for the house. They located an absolutely exceptional piece of land whose panoramas can only be described as views of heaven. 🌲 Once the purchase was finalized, roads had to be cut and power lines installed. An average of fifteen feet of snow accumulates here during the winter, and the building site is located above eight thousand feet, so the building had to be able to withstand

Overlooking a spectacular mountain and ski range, the Roddy Lodge is situated among stands of lodgepole pines. It sits off a winding dirt road with hairpin turns in an area that gets an average of fifteen feet of snow each winter.

almost torturous environmental elements. Yellowstone Traditions was hired to construct the building. Interior designer

Carol Sisson was engaged to decorate the home. During my winter visit, upon arriving at the gatehouse we agreed that

we were very smart to have rented an oversized SUV with four-wheel drive. We spent about forty minutes traveling about

five miles along the freshly plowed private road. Elk were everywhere. Upon arriving at the house, a caretaker opened the

doors and welcomed us to Roddy Lodge, also known as Elk Run. Built in old-world style, the house received great care

to insure that the texture, hue, richness, and color of the materials used in construction enhanced the subtle ambiance

sought by the owners. Using only recycled materials, including dead-standing timbers, the builders, architects, interior

designers, and owners sought absolute simplicity in the project. Masons constructed the base of native alpine stone to tol-

The dining area has space for a large dining table made of Douglas fir by Tod Gardiner of Yellowstone Traditions. The old-world chairs, built specifically for this house, were covered with rich red kilim carpets. Antler chandelier by Frank Long.

To enhance the European appearance, the owners hired Jennifer Bessen to paint medieval scenes on the hallway walls. Considerable effort was taken to find and use highly textured materials, such as logs and barn boards, to enhance the setting.

erate the extreme conditions often found in the region. Although the home appears to be constructed of logs, the structure is actually a framed house sided with half-round logs.

The interior logs were all hand-colored and -waxed to enhance the warm hues. The interior of the house also boasts several extraordinary examples of original design while the exterior benefited from construction innovations such as an engineered frame structure and a full-wrapped log and stone exterior. The logs for the entire home were cut on the property. The result is an astonishingly warm home so charming, comfortable, and inviting that I had to stop for several moments to reflect on the creativity of the human race.

One sitting area of the Roddy
Lodge includes oversized burgundy soft-leather armchairs.
Oriental rugs, many featuring
rich reds, are used to add life to
the earth tones consistent
throughout the structure.

*Built-in bookcases
made from barn wood
act as display cases in
this combination room.*

The façade of the bar is lined with half-round dead-standing lodgepole pine poles. The Hammerton Company of Salt Lake City made the elk-motif bar stools and hanging arch.

The refrigerator façade was covered with copper. The owners, who often have large numbers of houseguests, utilize a large industrial range.

A fireplace warms the master bedroom, where a striking rustic staircase leads to an upper balcony.

The barn wood to
the right of the easy
chair (below the
extraordinary rustic
staircase) hides a
high-tech entertain-
ment center.

Furnishings in the master suite reflect a Spanish motif. The walls have been textured and sponge-painted a soft yellow.

The wash area off the master bath contains handmade cabinetry and a striking ceiling made of rugged lodgepole branches.

A view of the living room provides a closer look at the highly textured logs, used here as beams and pillars.

Another bathroom in the home contains this unique root-base washstand made of lodgepole pine.

This simple washstand was made of antique barn boards and a drop-in copper sink. The walls were sponge-painted rust red.

All the doors in the home were hand-made from locally cut wood. Each door is an original creation.

Built-in bunk beds and bureaus meet the needs of the many grandkids and their guests who visit the home.

A floor-to-ceiling view of the master bedroom shows the Arts & Crafts wall sconces and ceiling fan.

An exterior view of the structure displays the extension of highly organic material to the outdoor balcony.

Victorian House
on an Adirondack Lake

BUILT TO LOOK OLD, rugged and rustic, the exterior of this structure nestled on the shores of an isolated lake in Adirondack State Park was covered with highly textured bark-on hemlock siding, arranged in geometric patterns. The home is unique in that much of the furnishings, accessories, and textiles originated during the Victorian period. The homeowner added life and depth to the house with layers and layers of textiles and charming displays of collectibles.

Surrounded by lush greenery and mature northern trees, this contemporary home was designed and built to appear "old-world rustic." Bark-on hemlock siding covers the year-round home.

The parlor dining room, overlooking the lake, is all decked out with a superb collection of Victorian china, glassware, and cutlery. The hanging glass lamp is from the turn of the century. The dining armchairs are made of hickory and date from the 1930s. Coyote skins cover the backs of several chairs.

A massive floor-to-ceiling fireplace provides warmth during the long Adirondack winter nights. The owner decorated the home with collections of high-style Victorian furnishings and accessories. The walls are knotty pine.

George Jacques created this bedside table, which features a stump base and mosaic top. Muted, layered textiles cover the bed.

The Adirondack sideboard was made by George Jacques. An outstanding collection of sterling silver accessories is prominently displayed. The armchairs are covered with paisley fabric.

A huge moose head hangs over
the massive stone fireplace.
A birch bark box rests on one
corner of the hearth and a
stuffed beaver on the other.

Jackson Fishing Retreat

OUTSIDE OF JACKSON, WYOMING, off a long, dusty dirt road lies a stretch of land that borders the Snake River. Famous for its abundance of cutthroat trout, the river and surrounding scenery draw individuals from all over the world. Elk, moose, bear, and deer are seemingly behind just about every tree. Hidden off the beaten path in a thicket of lodgepole pine, the medium-sized log cabin is filled with rustic treasures. ☞ When compared to other homes, this cabin may seem small in size but its comfortable ambiance is immediately apparent upon first entering.

Both eastern and western furnishings mix comfortably in this home. The living room set consists of several historical pieces made by Thomas Molesworth in the 1930s. The western branding-iron chandelier was designed by and purchased from Fighting Bear Antiques.

The dining room set was also made by Molesworth in the 1930s. A collection
of antique Black Forest wall hangers brings in a bit of European flavor.

Barney Bellinger of Sampson Bog Studios created this striking boathouse cabinet. Known for incorporating unique rustic items such as the oars in this piece, Bellinger's work is often the centerpiece of major collections throughout the country.

Detail of a painting on an accessory piece by Barney Bellinger, who is perhaps the best-known and most creative East Coast rustic artist.

Nestled between two Thomas Molesworth club chairs, this yellow birch stump-based floor lamp speaks of the freedom of nature.

In the corner of an upstairs bedroom rests this chest by Barney Bellinger. His furniture, often adorned with his original paintings, is both functional and artistic.

This striking bed by Barney Bellinger incorporates hundreds of burls from lodgepole pines. Bellinger also superbly crafted in birch bark, acorns, and antique fly-fishing memorabilia.

Located in a corner off the dining room rests
this small, yellow birch, stump-based table.
The top is highly figured bird's-eye maple and
the base includes antlers from fallow deer.

Painting detail on the root-based table by Barney Bellinger.

Big Hole River Ranch

THE WATER WAS LOW IN THE BIG HOLE RIVER; drought had taken its toll. We had driven down a dirt road more than an hour without seeing another car. Nothing but high mountain desert, tumbleweeds, pronghorn antelope, mule deer, and an occasional stand of cottonwood trees dotted the landscape. Dry and gray was the order of the day. ⤙⤘ Pulling into a gated driveway that was the entrance to the Big Hole River Ranch in the wilds of Montana, we noticed a small pond surrounded by a manicured green lawn and a few mature hardwood trees. I parked the car and we wandered over for a few minutes of relaxation by the cool, clear water. After a few minutes I noticed the telltale signs of rising fish. Moments later my three-year-old daughter came wandering up to me with a bucket of fish pellets she had found under a nearby tree. I took a handful of pellets and tossed them nonchalantly into the water. ⤙⤘ We were shocked at what we saw: like starving sharks, more than a hundred rainbow trout, most in the thirty-inch range, churned the waters and devoured the pellets in seconds. My next handfuls brought more and more trout. Dangling my bare toes or swimming in the pond was out of the question. We went through the bucket and then halfway through a fifty-pound bag of trout feed before I thought of my fly rod sitting patiently in the SUV. "No problem," said the caretaker, "fish all you want."

This cabin, part of a complex of camps made of recycled materials, occupies a tract of land that includes more than two miles of waterfront on the Big Hole River. A small drain stream runs directly in front of the cabin.

The traditionally furnished cabin comes complete with a stone fireplace, large windows, and built-in storage space.

But reason prevailed. We were there to take photos and the sun was low in the west, just above the mountains. We returned to the vehicle, drove another hundred yards, and parked in front of one of numerous inviting log cabins. Designed by architect Larry Pearson in the image of "Rocky Mountain sour dough cabins of the 1800s," the structure was built by Yellowstone Traditions out of dead-standing lodgepole pine trees and locally dismantled historical cabins. Construction superintendent Justin Bowland sought absolute simplicity and authenticity in the cabin design and used pioneer AV notches to join the logs together at corners. The complex of several small cabins and a larger main dining and meeting hall, sitting significantly off the beaten path, blended perfectly with the nearby mountains and high-desert scrub environment. Built as a fishing retreat, the camp is jointly owned and maintained by a small group of fly-fishing enthusiasts from around the country. The owners of the cabin shown here acted as interior designers for the building and provided the furnishings and artwork from their own collection.

A mahogany dining room set
serves as both an eating space
and display area for the owners'
ever-changing collection of
bronzes and other artwork.
A small kitchenette sits off the
dining area. The arch over
the doorway was cut from
dead-standing lodgepole pine.

The living room features green leather sofas along with collections of bronzes and artwork. To bring out the richness in the wood, each log is hand-finished and -waxed.

Another view of the dining area, including
a moose-antler chandelier designed by
contractors Yellowstone Traditions.

The bedroom includes a king-sized bed
constructed in southwestern style.
Numerous built-in shelves house an
extensive collection of antique decoys
and other fishing memorabilia.

A second bathroom is complete with an antique barn-board vanity, a custom fly-fishing mirror, and hand-carved fish.

A bathroom off the bedroom was made of recycled material, and the countertop is covered with tiles.

To maintain simplicity and authenticity, the corners of the building
are comprised of staggered-length AV notches.

Standing Bear Lodge

THIS CLASSIC ADIRONDACK MOUNTAIN HOME was designed to showcase the rustic furniture of George Jacques. George is a long-established rustic furniture builder in the Adirondacks and retired state patrol officer. George and Mary Jacques, owners of the home, designed the setting with architect Will Forester. It is constructed of white pine, and the stones for the massive fireplace were dug from Johns Brook, also on the Jacques property. As with many rustic homes, the front of the house is oriented toward the view so that one approaches and enters the house from the rear. This four-bedroom, three-bath home has five thousand feet of living space. The home is a statement of modern conveniences and rustic simplicity.

Comfortable in both function and form, this Adirondack home is a fusion of modern conveniences and contemporary rustic furnishings. The massive fireplace was made from locally dug fieldstones and extends to the ceiling. A massive moose-antler chandelier illuminates the living room.

The homeowners chose upholstered furniture covered with burgundy leather or tapestry. Strong colors, especially reds, are good complements to log structures, which often are overburdened with the natural color of wood. A collection of Adirondack accessories and taxidermy rests on the mantel.

A large section of windows allows light to brighten the dwelling,

which stands in the dense woods of the northern Adirondacks.

Most of the home is classic post-and-beam construction, while

logs outline many of the angles. The ceiling is knotty pine.

An overview of the kitchen reveals a countertop covered with granite. The kitchen floor and cabinets are cherry wood. A 1920s oak icebox resides in one corner of the room.

The façade and sides of the kitchen island are covered with bark from white birch trees. The bar stools are made of hickory.

Rustic furniture maker George Jacques created the dining room table and classic Adirondack birch sideboard. Amish builders in upstate New York constructed the side chairs made of hickory poles. The chairs are woven with the inner material of the rattan plant. Most of the walls throughout the home are painted a soft yellow.

This table was made from the stump of a
yellow birch tree. The tabletop is highly
figured lace wood. The canoe paddles are
from the early 1900s.

It's easy to imagine the hot breath of a bear while reading an adventure novel in this overstuffed armchair.

This small cabinet is actually an entertainment center. The doors open to display a large-screen TV and other electronic equipment.

This stark hallway setting is graced with a narrow sofa table made by George Jacques.

This classic birch armchair was made by rustic artist Jack Leadley. A legend in the Adirondacks, Leadley works in the style pioneered by Lee Fountain in the 1930s to produce both armchairs and rockers made of yellow birch. Leadley not only makes the chairs but hand weaves the seats and backs from locally cut black ash trees.

A tall chest made by George Jacques is just right for this bedroom. The polar bear rug is to be avoided when wandering around in the dark.

Rocky Mountain Luxury

WHEN I FIRST WALKED INTO THIS Colorado Rocky Mountain home, I felt I was in a cathedral. Having the ambiance and spirit of many of the old national park lodges, the home is a study in western character and modern technology. It's located in a gated community on the side of a mountain and within eyesight of other vacation homes, where the views of the surrounding mountains are spectacular. To the credit of the design team—the architectural firm of Robertson, Miller and Terrell and interior designer Melissa Greenauer of the Greenauer Group—the casualness and comfort of the home are immediately evident. It was the desire of the client that the home appear to have been lived in for many years and that authentic western artifacts and textiles be used whenever possible. Entering through a ground-floor entrance, the foyer and hallway walls are windowless walls of stone. Climbing a grand staircase, one enters a highly dramatic world designed for comfort and to impress—which, without being presumptuous, it clearly does!

Overview of the living room and grand staircase. Built with massive logs, the home has a standard of uniqueness and comfort not often found in homes of this scale. The chandeliers, handmade by Rosebud Forge of Lajara, Colorado, incorporate antique branding irons. Arts & Crafts—style pillows were used throughout the house.

Accessory pieces such as birch bark canoes, antler table lamps, and moose heads add to the rustic flavor of the home.

*Interior designer Melissa Greenauer often incorporates pots
filled with dried plants. Lester Santos of Cody, Wyoming,
made the armchair with tan leather cushions.*

Opposite: A buffalo head hangs over the dramatic fireplace. Brightly colored geometric rugs provide needed contrast to the background neutrals.

A group of shelves for books, bottles, and other collectibles lines one side of the fireplace. A wide variety of textiles were used in the setting. The casual leather lampshade on the floor lamp says "relax."

The leather-covered
armchair and
ottoman were made
by Lester Santos.

Designed to blend with both the logs and stones, the upholstered furniture incorporates colors of tan and brown, and a few leopard spots! The many throw pillows add comfort and a sense of casualness. The even-arm settles, made from lodgepole pine, were designed by Melissa Greenauer.

The massive fireplaces can be enjoyed from both the living room and dining areas. The old-world Spanish-style chairs are covered with leather.

The spindles of the grand staircase are from locally cut hardwoods. A colorful antique American flag makes a statement.

*In the evenings the sun
streams through the
windows, illuminating the
entire setting. It brings
back memories of national
parks, grand lodges, and
rugged wilderness.*

A chaise lounge handmade by Dan McPhail has elk-antler feet. It provides a display place for souvenir pillows and teddy bears.

A rock-sheathed bathtub provides the bather with magical transport to natural pools and waterfalls. At sunset, golden light pours through the window.

Winter Terrace Ski House

RESTING ON A WOODED SLOPE near the Grand Tetons in Wyoming sits this contemporary rustic home. Designed by architect Eliot Goss of Jackson, Wyoming, and built by Teton Heritage Builders, the house was decorated by interior designer Cheryl Gallinger of Gallinger/Trauner Design. The home, called Winter Terrace, is located on the foothills of a major ski resort. The owners can ski right to their front door directly from the slopes. Although not a huge home, the structure was decorated to allow for easy traffic flow. In other words, the home is not a receptacle for unnecessary clutter. Each vignette in the home, whether for dining, living or entertainment, is carefully laid out to accommodate casual wandering. Further, the angles within the interior of the structure take on a life unto themselves. The inner perspectives from just about any view are original, challenging, and creative. Views from both the front and back of the house are exceptional.

This designer home is illuminated with Arts & Crafts lighting. Built in classic
mountain style and engineered to withstand the tremendous snow loads of the Teton
Mountains, the home blends comfortably with its surrounding environment.

A hand-stitched leather couch rests in front of a massive fireplace. The toss pillows are covered with muted tree-tone materials as well as Indian textiles. Classic Indian patterns were incorporated into the hand-forged hardware that secures the structural logs to each other.

Above: The dining room set, created by Bohlmann Pine Designs, was constructed from dead-standing lodgepole pine. The two end chairs and benches are covered with buffalo hides.

Tim Groth created these club chairs, which serve as seating in front of a rustic entertainment center. The chairs are made from locally cut pine trees. An antique Navajo carpet provides color.

The casters on the chair legs of this unique rustic dining room set allow for easy maneuvering on the oak floor. The dining set was made by Scottsdale Art Factory.

This high-tech kitchen has all the latest electronic gadgets. Tim Groth built the bar stools. The kitchen ceiling is partially covered with embossed tin.

*The island and countertops,
as well as back splashes,
are covered with stone.*

An overview of the living room shows the fireplace and exposed structural log beams. A minimal use of accessories creates a casual atmosphere in the setting.

A bar table, stools, and a pool table were built by Draw Knife for the downstairs recreation room. Like many of the pieces in the Rocky Mountains, the items were made from lodgepole pine and juniper trees.

The canopy bed was made from lodgepole pine, abundant throughout the Rocky Mountains. Heavy earth-tone textiles cover the bed.

An original 1930s desk by Thomas Molesworth provides a study area. The extraordinary armchair and ottoman, created by Red Bird, are covered with leather hides.

A small room off the kitchen holds a designer settee made by Brad Andes from lodgepole pine. The setting is complete with cowboy accessories and a bearskin rug on the floor.

Another bedroom is the setting for this large queen-sized bed made from lodgepole pine.

The bunkroom is complete with bunk beds made from highly figured lodgepole. Colorful ticking material covers the beds.

This ornate mosaic armoire was created by Bohlmann Pine Designs.

A downstairs bedroom contains this fireplace, built of fieldstone, and a club chair covered in hair-on cowhide. Chair by Tim Groth.

A Minimalist Rustic Apartment

THIS APARTMENT RESIDENCE IS LOCATED on the second floor of a new log home. But the first floor isn't functioning as a home—it's a retail business. The main floor has a cozy fireplace and is also connected to a greenhouse/sunroom. To protect the peacefulness of the second-floor bedrooms from potential street noise below, the bedrooms are on the back side of the building while the living room is on the front. A high-end collection of American Indian and western items stand out against the white walls in a room otherwise decorated in minimalist style.

Doors handcrafted of local antique barn board are graced by a stained-glass window utilizing an Arts & Crafts pattern.

The Black Forest bear hall tree was made in Switzerland. Cabinets like this yellow one were typically produced in the Midwest around the turn of the century.

The dining table and side chairs are Gustav Stickley originals. The partnering of wood furniture pieces and colorful Navajo rugs makes a bold statement of quality craftsmanship in this room. The large chestnut cabinet on the left wall, circa 1900, is a rare find since a blight made chestnut hard to find by the middle 1910s.

For the classic log cabin interior, the owners chose a complementary post-and-beam construction. The dining room set, sideboard, and small table are original Gustav Stickley pieces. Antique Indian rugs add drama to the home. The cats are Himalayan.

Built-in display cabinets provide shelving for pottery and other Indian artifacts. The soft green upholstered furniture and earth-toned carpets coordinate perfectly with the dead-standing timber used throughout the house.

The small kitchenette has custom cabinets made of cherry.

Rustic artist Albert Gabbey created this mosaic sideboard in the 1920s. Mosaic work had its origins in Europe centuries ago and was first introduced to North America in the Adirondacks in the early 1800s. This antique piece was created from locally cut Rocky Mountain softwoods. The large antique basket is Apache.

A Gustav Stickley sideboard acts as both a server during meals and a display space for western collectibles. The dramatic antique navy blue-and-red Indian blanket in the foreground is Teec-Nos-Pos. The hammered-copper lamps, lined with mica in the shades, are classic Arts & Crafts items from the early 1900s.

Display cases house part of an extensive collection of Indian artifacts, including kachina dolls. The side chair was made by Thomas Molesworth in the 1930s.

Condos and Modern Homes

NOT EVERYONE LIKES LOG CABINS. Some people find them to be too primitive, difficult to clean, and outside the realm of their taste. Nonetheless, during the past few years, even sophisticates have recognized the inherent beauty in rustic furnishings and have added rustic elements to such modern residences as condominiums, townhouses, and contemporary residences other than log structures—and with good reason. Many rustic furniture makers around the country have elevated the level of their craft to the profound. Besides, rustic furniture is inherently fun. It's casual and relaxing. It's wild and free and not to be taken too seriously under any circumstances. Its lack of pretension does away with convention and can immediately render one humble! 🌳 The next several pages include photos of dwellings that are not rustic by nature. Nonetheless, several of the homeowners, as a concession to "rustic," may have included interior log walls or log beams.

This condominium dining room with Stickley spindle chairs is complimented by a rustic Lester Santos juniper chandelier with mica shades.

This traditional home is greatly enhanced by wood beams, a rustic coffee table, and a cut-off canoe bookshelf. The leather couches and original artwork add to the ambience and comfort of the home.

A white wall shows off a Barney Bellinger Angler's Chest. Bellinger builds traditional furnishings innovatively and adorns his pieces with rustic items such as paddles, oars, and fishing poles. Bellinger is also an accomplished Adirondack painter; his paintings, as seen on this bureau, are his signature feature on furniture compositions.

This stark condominium setting shows off the lines of a classic western sofa designed and built by Lester Santos. The cushions are leather and the sofa is made of cherry and juniper.

Rustic artist Doug Tedrow created the twig fireplace mantel in this Idaho townhouse. The acrylic cement hearth was fashioned and sponge-painted by artist Jack Burgess. The metal firescreen was made by Jim Gibson. The warm yellow sponge-painted walls create an ideal backdrop for the several pieces of high-end rustic furniture throughout the house.

A small cabin on Lake George holds this creative sofa table by Chris Wager. The top is highly figured quartersawn oak. The base contains moose antlers and roots from yellow birch trees. The photo above the table is from the 1920s. The antique pack baskets were generally made from the splint of black ash trees and have been part of Adirondack lore for generations.

The entryway into this townhouse is the setting for a chip-carved sideboard and mirror by Doug Tedrow. The sideboard shows the influence of the Reverend Ben Davis, who lived and preached (and built furniture) in North Carolina in the early part of the twentieth century. Tedrow made the sconces based on a Barney Bellinger design.

*Tim Groth created this comfortable-looking chaise
lounge. Tim is well known in the West for his creative
designs and high-quality upholstery. The firescreen
was made by Jack Burgess.*

A collection of antique Old Hickory pieces graces a corner of the author's home. The floor lamp and comb-back rocker date around 1910. The dark green curtains are rustic in motif. The curtain rods are yellow birch poles, and the hardware was created from deer antlers.

A condo loft in New Hampshire is brought to life by a collection of antique fishing creels and other rustic memorabilia.

Adirondack artist Peter Winter made this small cupboard.

*Opposite: This New York con-
dominium is enhanced by the
inclusion of traditional post-
and-beam wood rafters. The
settee under the staircase is by
Michael Hutton, who is well
known for his interesting and
creative interpretation of rustic
settees and other furnishings.*

*Made of quartersawn oak, this
small desk and chair serve as a
nightstand in a New York home.
Peter Winter made the two
pieces. The bark sticks are pieces
made of yellow birch.*

Interior decorator Melissa Greenauer designed this elegant Colorado setting.
Her use of soft natural colors, dried plants, and other natural materials create
remarkable settings for her many clients and projects.

This condominium entry is enhanced by a table and mirror by Chris Wager.

Barney Bellinger created this whimsical hallstand. It contains a classical Bellinger painting illuminated by a fifteen-watt bulb and an art-glass shade.

Peter Winter created this unusual sideboard, whose panels
are covered with white birch bark. The mosaic work
includes yellow birch twigs. Birch wood is harvested only
in winter, insuring the stability of the bark.

This New Hampshire condo office reflects the interests of the owner, who collects and sells antique rustic accessories.

An opposite view of the New Hampshire office includes a colorful collection of antique paddles, snowshoes, Adirondack pack baskets, and other rustic collectibles.

This entryway exemplifies the ability of rustic to blend with other styles. An art nouveau glass lamp stands atop a small rustic table by Chris Wager.

A classic Adirondack armchair by Tom Welsh employs antlers in a functional as well as decorative manner.

A fantastic rustic innovation, this hollow-log shelf was made by Brian Kelly.

The fancy hall mirror by rustic artist
Laurie Toledo and a sofa table by Peter
Winter make a gracious pairing.

This contemporary home with wood-paneled walls overlooks the wonderful waters of classic Adirondack Lake George. Adirondack builder Peter Winter made the birch bark and mosaic sideboard. The dark bark on the piece is actually the reverse side of white birch bark. The dining room chairs were designed by the author and made by the Old Hickory Furniture Company.

Rustic artist Peter Winter created this imposing entertainment center. Throughout the years, Peter has consistently produced creative pieces that grace many high-end Adirondack homes.

The octagonal stump-based table was created by Peter
Winter. The base is made of apple and beech branches.

Resources

Jack Burgess
Sculptures in Wood and Bronze
P.O. Box 2361
Sun Valley, ID 83353
208.726.2566
www.tiptable.com/Jack/
jackhome.html

Dan and Steve Butts
High Country Designs
P.O. Box 5656
720 Main Street
Frisco, CO 80443
970.668.0109
970.668.4592 fax
placer@colorado.net
www.highcountrydesigns.com

Mark Catman
Birchbark Designs
47 Main Street
East Berne, NY 12059
518.872.9614

Chris Chapman
Chapman Design
0075 Deer Trail Avenue
Carbondale, CO 81623
970.963.9580
970.963.0228 fax

Stephen Chisholm
High Ridge Rustics
13 Old County Road
Waterford, VT 05848

Phil Clausen
Clausen Studio
93937 Hwy 42 South at Riverton
Coquille, OR 97423
541.396.4806

Diane C. Ross
Rustic Furniture
P.O. Box 253
Willow Creek, MT 59760
406.285.6882
plentyponies@aol.com
www.rusticfurniture.net

Jimmy and Lynda Covert
Covert Workshops
2007 Public Street
Cody, WY 82414
307.527.5964 phone/fax

Marvin Davis and
Robert O'Leary
Romancing the Woods, Inc.
33 Raycliff Drive
Woodstock, NY 12498
914.246.1020
914.246.1021 fax
davis@rtw-inc.com
www.rtw-inc.com

Jerry and Jessica Farrell
Box 255
Sidney Center, NY 13839
607.369.4916

Peter Fillerup
Wild West Designs
P.O. Box 286
Heber, UT 84032
435.654.4151
435.654.1653 fax
peter@wildwestdesigns.com
www.wildwestdesigns.com

John Gallis
Norseman Designs West
38 Road 2AB
Cody, WY 82414
307.587.7777

Thomas George
SweetTree Rustic
P.O. Box 1827
Tonasket, WA 98855
509.486.1573

Jim Gibson
Gibson & Gibson
Antique Lighting
Chula Vista, CA 91911
619.422.2447
619.422.2495 fax

Glenn Gilmore,
Architectural Blacksmith
Gilmore Metalsmithing Studio
P.O. Box 961
Hamilton, MN 59840
406.961.1861
glenn@gilmoremetal.com
www.gilmoremetal.com

Tim Groth
PMB 158
111 Broadway, Suite 133
Boise, ID 83702
208.338.0331
208.424.0545 fax

Chris Hauver
The Woodsmith
364 Hopkins Hill Road
Coventry, RI 02816
401.826.7321

Hilary Heminway
and Terry Baird
Montana Wagons
P.O. Box 1
McLeod, MT 59052
406.932.4350 or
860.535.3110

Randy Holden
Elegantly Twisted
73 East Dyer Street
Skowhegan, ME 04976
207.474.7507

Michael Hutton
Twig Mosaic Creations
RR2, Box 162
Pittsfield, IL 62363
217.285.5277
alice@adams.net
homepages.msn.com/Commercial
St/alicedad/surprise.html

Wayne Ignatuk
Rustic Woodworks
55 Trumbulls Corner Road
Jay, NY 12941
518.946.7439

Amber Jean
1106 West Park, #268
Livingston, MT 59047
406.222.9251
amber@amberjean.com
www.amberjean.com

Stephen Kent and Joan Benson
Crystal Farm Antler
Chandeliers and Furniture
18 Antelope Road
Redstone, CO 81623
970.963.2350
970.963.0709 fax
cfarm@rof.net

David Laitinen
New World Endeavors
P.O. Box 286
McAllister, MT 59740
406.580.2395

Jack Leadley
Leadley's Adirondack Sugar Bush
P.O. Box 142
Speculator, NY 12164
518.548.7093

Dan MacPhail Antler Studio
1645 McKendree Church Road
Kevil, KY 42053
270.488.2522
bear@apex.com

Matt Madsen and Tim Duncan
Burl Art Productions
P.O. Box 187
Orick, CA 95555
707.488.3795
707.488.3565 fax
burlart@juno.com

Brent McGregor &
Kara Mickaelson
Rocky Mountain Timber
Products
Box 1477
Sisters, OR 97759
541.549.1322

Clifton Monteith
P.O. Box 9
Lake Ann, MI 49650
231.275.6560 phone/fax
monteithc@aol.com

John Mortensen
The Rainbow Trail Collection
P.O. Box 746
Wilson, WY 83014
307.733.1519
307.733.5216 fax
mortensen@rmisp.com
www.mortensenstudios.com

Nick Nickerson
P.O. Box 618
Copake, NY 12516
518.329.1665

Old Hickory Furniture Company
403 South Noble Street
Shelbyville, IN 46176
800.232.2275 toll-free
317.392.6740 local
317.398.2275 fax
mail@oldhickory.com
www.oldhickory.com

J. Mike Patrick
New West
2811 Big Horn Avenue
Cody, WY 82414
800.653.2391 toll-free
307.587.2839 local
307.527.7409 fax
jmike@newwest.com
www.newwest.com

Andy Sanchez
Custom Furniture by
Andy Sanchez
205 Main Street
Belen, NM 87002
888.212.7722 toll-free
505.864.2003 phone/fax
customfurniture@specialtymile.com
www.specialtymile.com/
customfurniture

Lester Santos
Santos Furniture Company
2208 Public Street
Cody, WY 82414
888.966.3489 toll-free
307.587.6543 local
307.527.4407 fax
lester@santosfurniture.com
www.santosfurniture.com

Jim Schreiner
P.O. Box 1407
Lake Placid, NY 12946
518.523.7081

Ron and Jean Shanor
Wildewood Furniture Company
P.O. Box 1631
Cody, WY 82414
877.208.4524 toll-free
307.587.9558
307.527.7247 fax

Doug and Janis Tedrow
Wood River Rustics
P.O. Box 3446
Ketchum, ID 83340
208.726.1442
208.726.1430 fax

Norman West
Spirit of the West Log Furniture
C-238
108 Ranch, BC V0K 2Z0
CANADA
250.791.5793

Ollie Burgess
Specialty Wood Products, Inc.
Mill Street
Bloomingdale, NY 12986
518.891.9149
518.891.2311 fax

Hank Ingram
Box 2552
Cody, WY 82414
307.527.7462
ingram@myavista.com
www.burlweb.com

Marty McCurry
Highland Craftsmen
P.O. Box 2011
151 Pine Street
Blowing Rock, NC 28605-2011
828.295.0796
highlandcraftsmen@boone.net
www.highlandcraftsmen.com

Northern Hardwoods
P.O. Box 308
Lake George, NY 12845
518.668.4501